Can You Drink a Dinosaur?

A Yes/No Book for Young Talkers

Written by a Speech-Language Pathologist

Cara Tambellini Danielson M.A. CCC-SLP

Illustrator: Mary Tambellini

ISBN-13: 978-0692833261I
ISBN-10: 0692833269

Message from the author:

I developed this book to get kids talking and thinking! With this book, children learn to answer questions, think critically about scenarios, and practice speaking in sentences. Children love answering the yes and no questions in this book. The predictable format allows for success (the first answer is always NO and the second is always YES). After reading this book several times with your child, you can have them practice answering the questions on their own. Even if your child answers YES when the answer should be NO, that is an opportunity for a fun dialogue between the reader and the child (e.g. "What?! I can throw an elephant? Okay I will try – too heavy!"). For children who aren't yet speaking in sentences, the last sentence of each page is an opportunity for them to practice their language skills. You can have your child repeat the last sentence or pause after saying "yes" and let your child "fill in" the last sentence on their own.

I hope you enjoy reading this book with your child!

Cara Tambellini Danielson M.A. CCC-SLP
caraspeechtherapy.com

Can you
eat a
house?

No

Can you eat an apple?

Yes

Eat an apple.

Can you throw an elephant?

No

Can you
throw a
ball?

Yes

Throw
the ball.

Can you drive a ladybug?

No

Can you drive a car?

Yes

Drive a car.

Can you
drink a
dinosaur?

No

Can you drink water?

Yes

Drink some water.

Can you wear ice cream?

No

Can you
wear a
coat?

Yes

Wear a
coat.

Can a puppy fly?

No

Can an
airplane
fly?

Yes

Fly the
airplane.

Made in the
USA
Middletown, DE